THE ALPS

THE

ALPS

SHIRO SHIRAHATA

© 1979 by Shiro Shirahata
Original edition published in Japanese by Yama-to Keikoku Sha Co., Ltd.

Published in English in the United States of America in 1980 by

RIZZOLI INTERNATIONAL PUBLICATIONS, INC.
712 Fifth Avenue / New York 10019

LC 80-50658

ISBN 0-8478-0316-3

Printed in Japan by
Dai Nippon Printing Co., Ltd., Tokyo

Contents

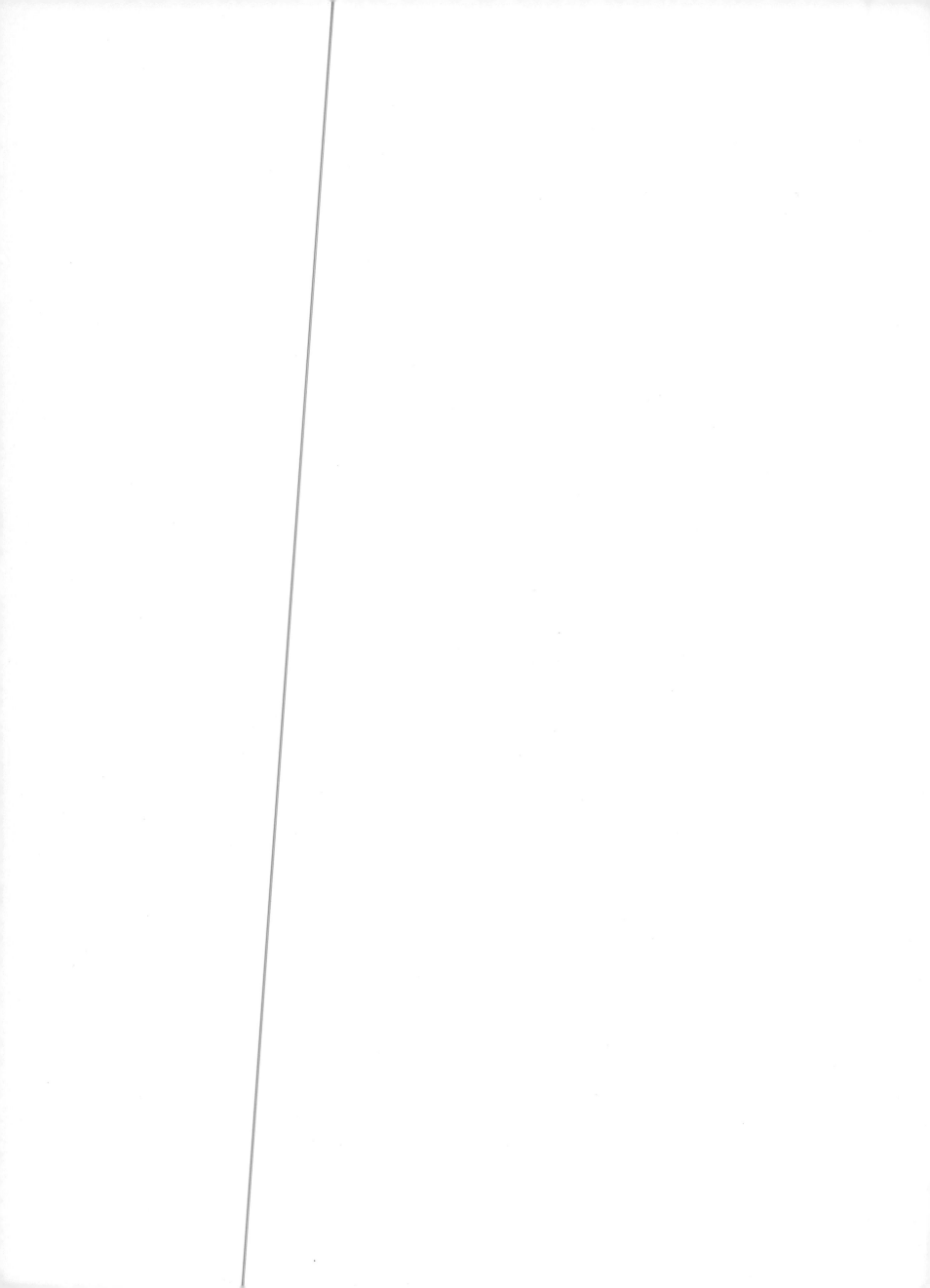

Preface

The Alps is the general name given to a complex system of mountain ranges which originates in Italy near San Remo, on the northern coast of the Mediterranean Sea. One hundred kilometers wide, with a total length of approximately twelve hundred kilometers, the Alps run northward in central Europe, in a roughly crescent shape, gradually turning east-northeast in the area west of Grenoble. Many national frontiers fall within the perimeter of this beautiful region, which encompasses parts of France, Italy, Switzerland, Germany, and Austria.

The three main divisions of Europe's Alps are the western, central, and eastern groups of ranges; these are divided still further into numerous groups and subgroups. The western area includes the Alpes du Dauphiné, also called le Massif des Ecrins, and the Alpes de Savoie. The famous Massif du Mont Blanc occurs within the latter range, and its size is such that it is considered a range in itself. The central Alps include the Wallis or Valais group, of which Monte Rosa is the highest peak, and the Berner Oberland, capped by Finsteraarhorn, and encompassing the massive Jungfrau, Eiger and Mönch. The eastern Alps include the Dolomiti range, with Marmolada the chief summit and Cortina d'Ampezzo the main town.

It would be virtually impossible to visit each of the countless mountains in the Alps, even if one had five or ten years to spend on such a project. Consequently, I limited my photographic excursions to le Massif du Mont Blanc, Berner Oberland, Alpi Bernina, the Wallis range, and the Dolomiti. For massive grandeur and soaring altitude, these five ranges surpass all others. I would have liked to include the Dauphiné range, but its remoteness and difficulty of access made me eliminate it from my itinerary.

In closing, I would like to thank Mr. Jiro Nitta, who helped me with advice and assistance in my travels to the Alps. I am also grateful to Mr. and Mrs. Garisch in Munich; to Mr. Yu Nakano and his wife, Mrs. Teruko Nakano, who accompanied me as my assistant on my travels in Europe; to Mr. Yasuhei Saito; to Mr. Suguru Suzuki of Chamonix; to Mr. and Mrs. Sekino and Miss Hideyo Sato; to the Yama-to Keikoku Sha Company, the Swiss Tourist Board, the Italian Tourist Board, and Mr. Henri Gaillard of the city of Chamonix; to the people of the Dai Nippon Printing Company; and above all, to Mr. Seiichi Tagawa, who was extremely helpful with the arrangement and layout of this book.

The kind assistance of these people, companies, and agencies made this book possible.

Shiro Shirahata

Le Massif du Mont Blanc

8

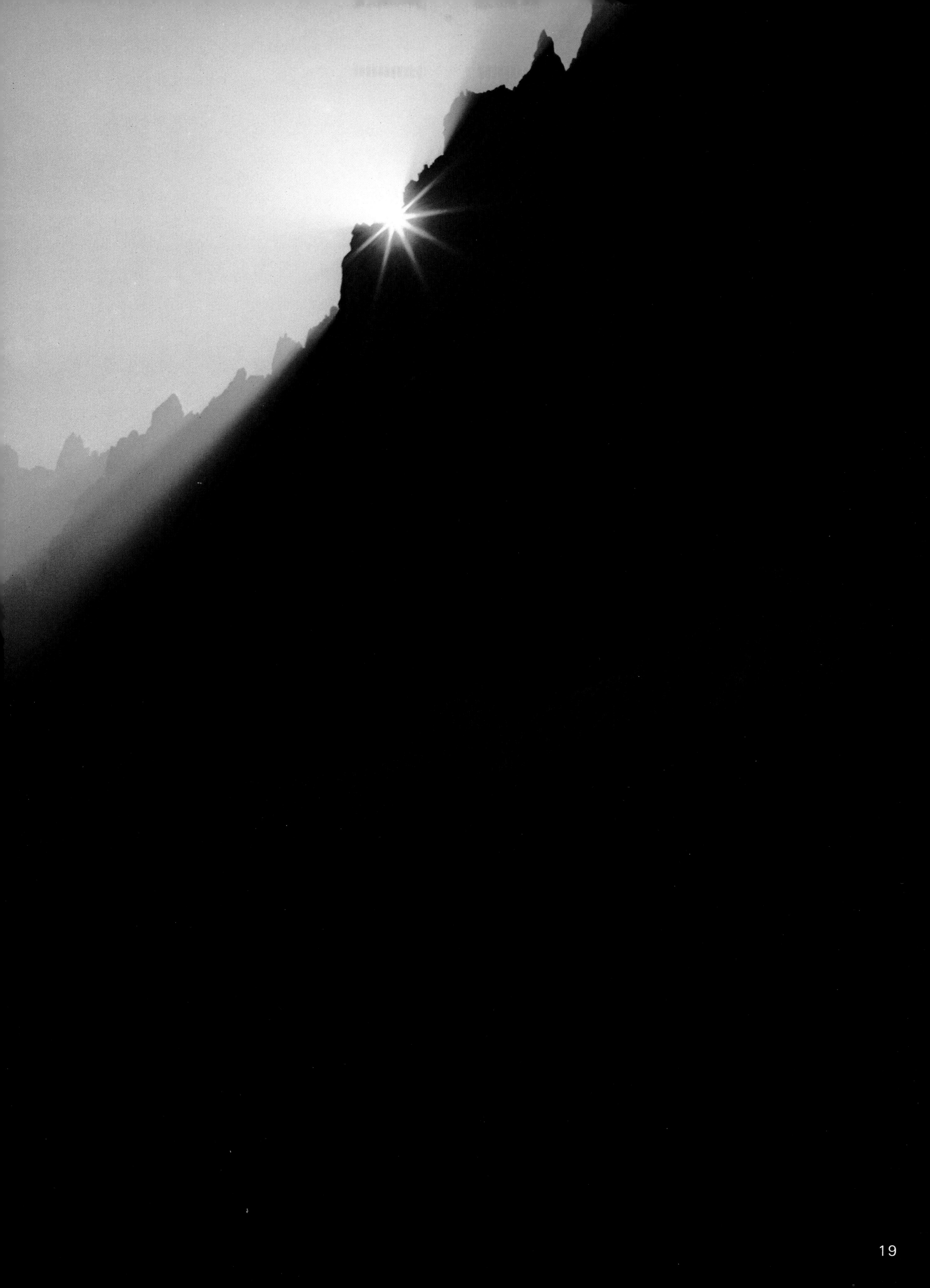

24

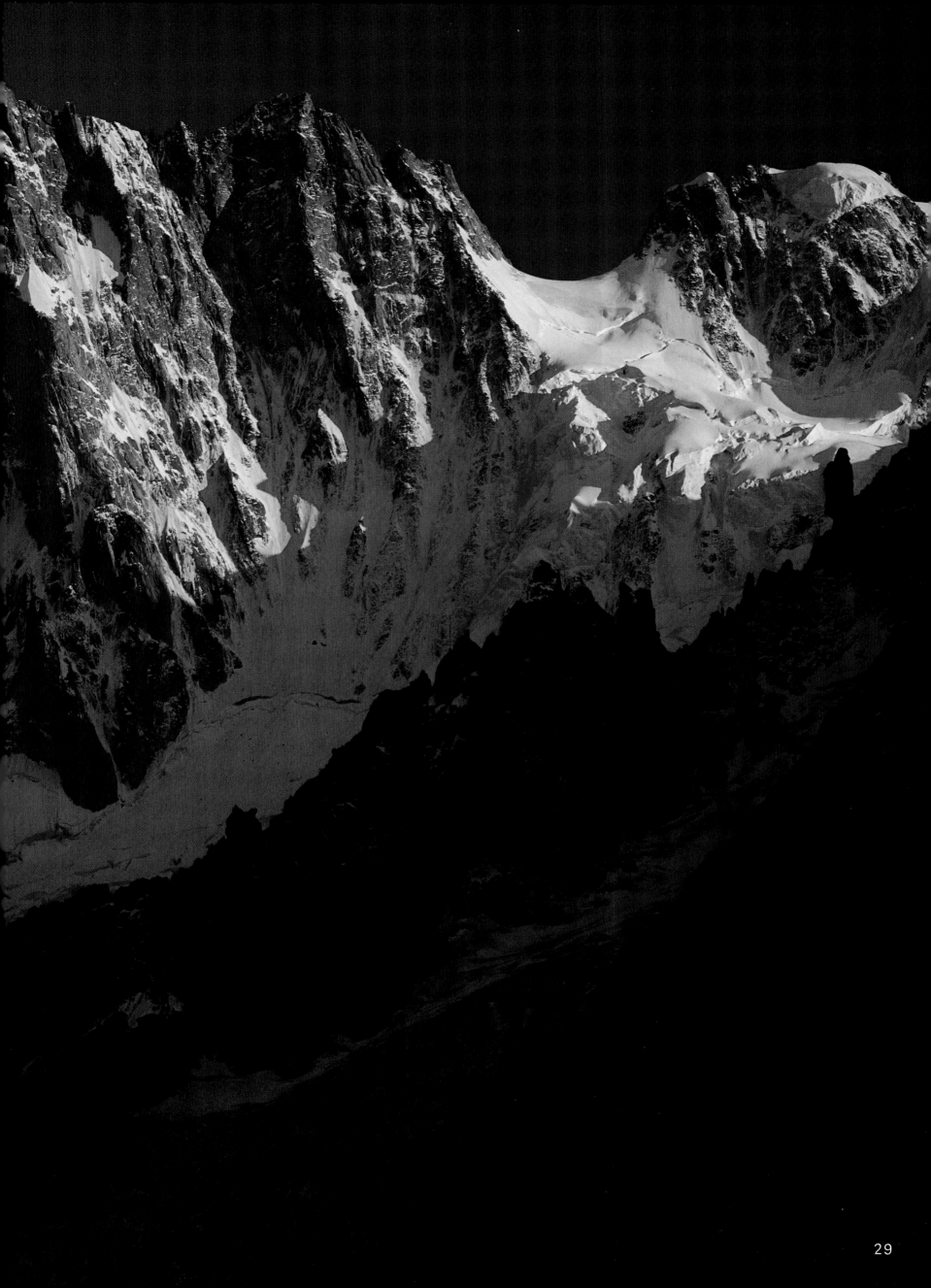

Wallis

Berner Oberland

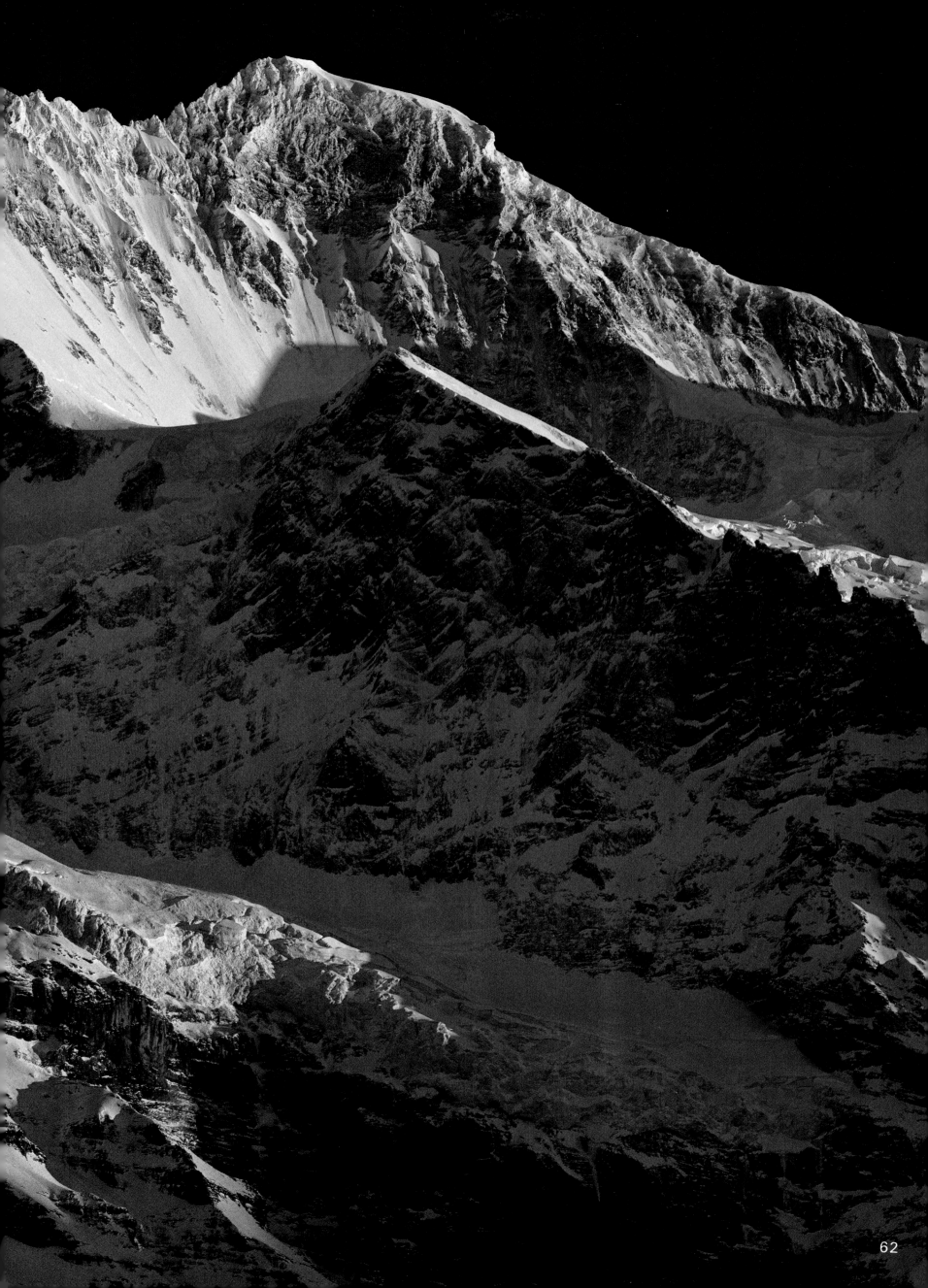

Alpi Bernina

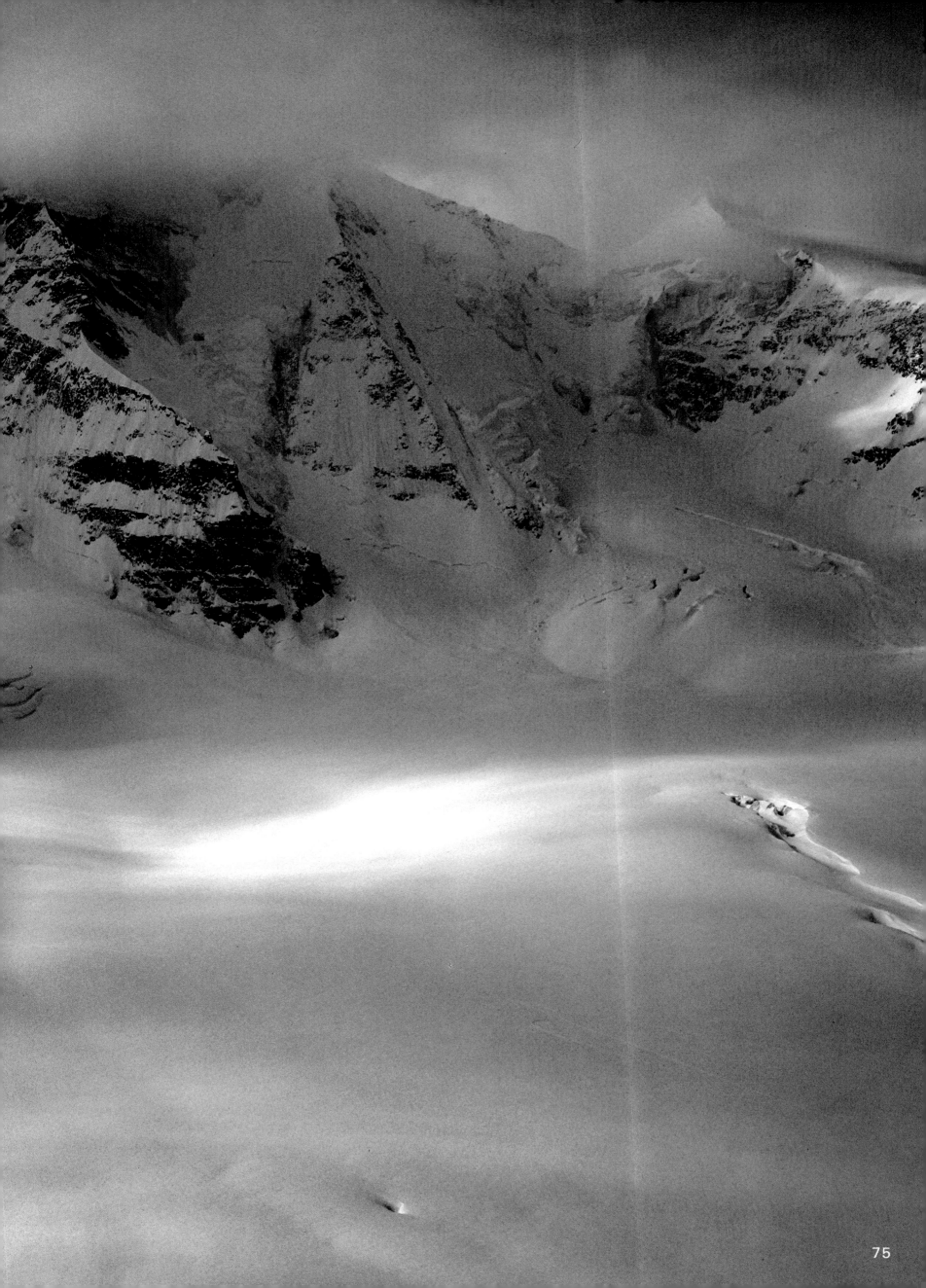

Dolomiti

93.

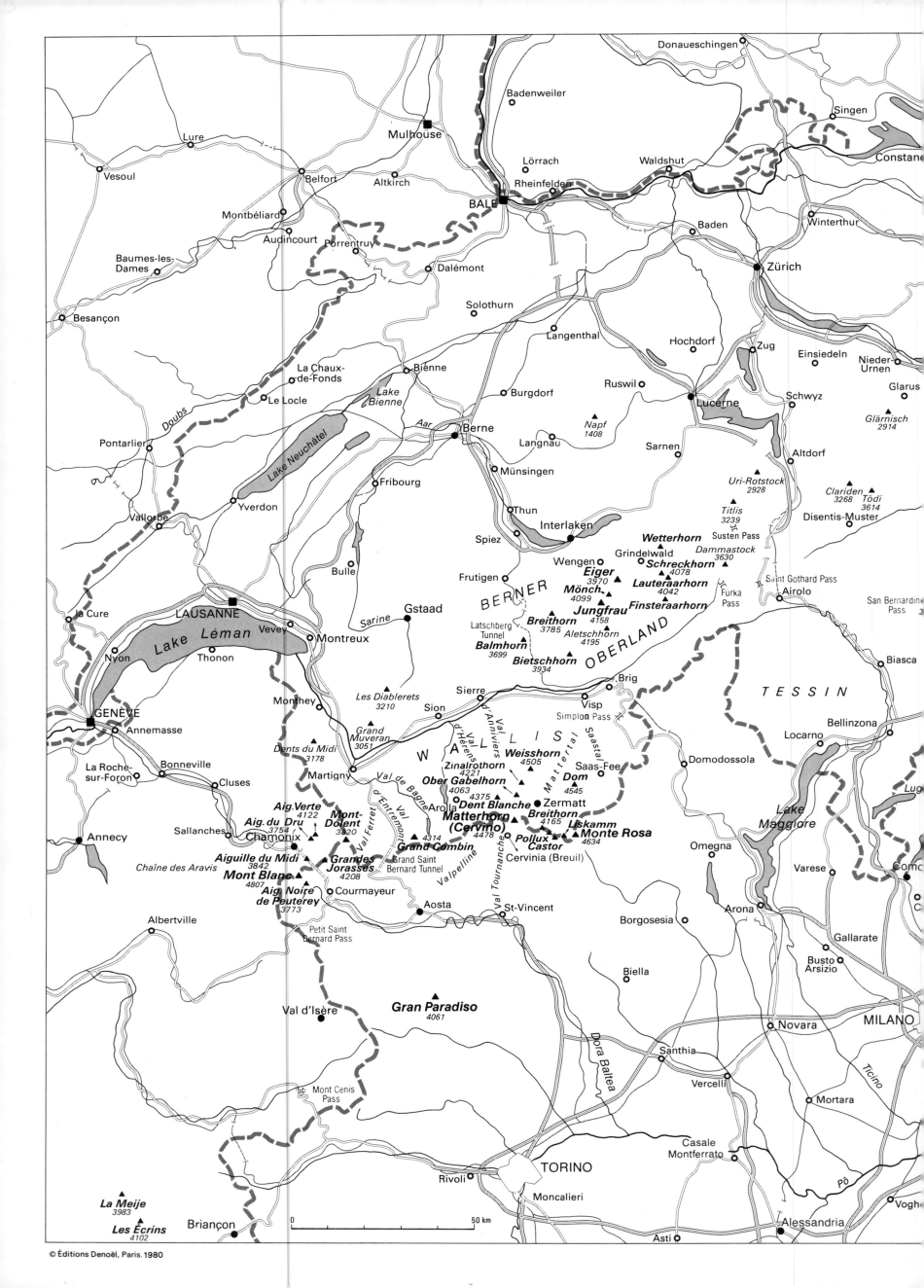

Donaueschingen

Singen

Badenweiler

Constance

Lörrach

Waldshut

Mulhouse

Lure

Altkirch

Rheinfelden

Baden

Winterthur

Vesoul

Belfort

BÂLE

Zürich

Montbéliard

Porrentruy

Audincourt

Dalémont

Solothurn

Baumes-les-
Dames

Besançon

Langenthal

Hochdorf

Zug

Einsiedeln

Nieder-
Urnen

La Chaux-
de-Fonds

Bienne

Burgdorf

Ruswil

Lucerne

Schwyz

Glarus

Le Locle

Lake
Bienne

Aar

Berne

*Napf
1408*

Sarnen

Altdorf

*Glärnisch
2914*

Doubs

Pontarlier

Lake Neuchâtel

Langnau

*Uri-Rotstock
2928*

*Clariden
3268*

*Tödi
3614*

Yverdon

Fribourg

Münsingen

*Titlis
3239*

Disentis-Muster

Vallorbe

Thun

Interlaken

Wetterhorn

Susten Pass

Saint Gothard Pass

Airolo

la Cure

Spiez

Wengen

Grindelwald

*Dammastock
3630*

Schreckhorn

San Bernardino
Pass

LAUSANNE

Vevey

Gstaad

Sarine

Frutigen

B E R N E R

*Eiger
3970*

Lauteraarhorn
4078

4042

Furka
Pass

Montreux

Mönch
4099

Jungfrau
4158

Finsteraarhorn

Lake Léman

Latschberg
Tunnel

Breithorn
3785

O B E R L A N D

Nyon

Thonon

Balmhorn
3699

*Aletschhorn
4195*

Biasca

Bietschhorn
3934

Brig

Monthey

*Les Diablerets
3210*

Sierre

Visp

T E S S I N

GENÈVE

Simplon Pass

Annemasse

Sion

Bellinzona

La Roche-
sur-Foron

Bonneville

*Grand
Muveran
3051*

W A L L I S

Weisshorn
4505

Saas-Fee

Locarno

Cluses

*Dents du Midi
3178*

Zinalrothorn
4221

Saastal

Dom
4545

Domodossola

Aig.Verte
4122

Martigny

**Ober
Gabelhorn**
4063

4375

Lake
Maggiore

Aig.du Dru
3754

**Mont-
Dolent**
3820

Arolla

Dent Blanche

Zermatt

Breithorn
4165

Sallanches

Chamonix

4314

**Matterhorn
(Cervino)**
4478

Liskamm

Annecy

Grand Combin

Pollux
Castor

Monte Rosa
4634

Omegna

Varese

Como

Aiguille du Midi
3842

**Grandes
Jorasses**
4208

Grand Saint
Bernard Tunnel

Cervinia (Breuil)

Chaîne des Aravis

Mont Blanc
4807

Courmayeur

St-Vincent

Arona

**Aig. Noire
de Peuterey**
3773

Aosta

Borgosesia

Albertville

Petit Saint
Bernard Pass

Biella

Gallarate

Busto
Arsizio

Val d'Isère

Gran Paradiso
4061

Novara

MILANO

Santhia

Dora Baltea

Vercelli

Mortara

Ticino

Mont Cenis
Pass

Casale
Montferrato

TORINO

Rivoli

Moncalieri

Pò

*La Meije
3983*

Asti

Alessandria

Briançon

*Les Écrins
4102*

0   50 km

Vogh

© Éditions Denoël, Paris. 1980

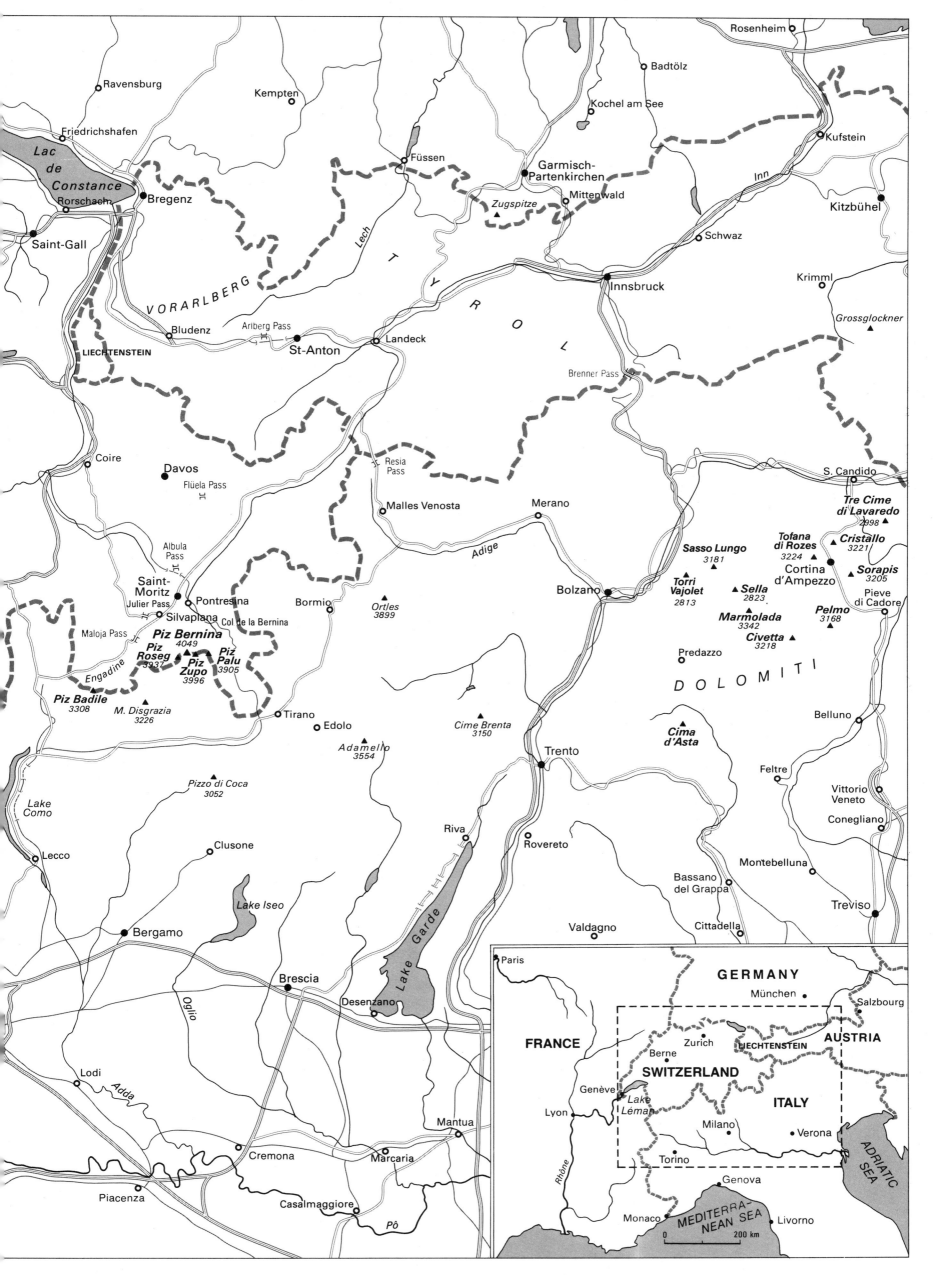

Le Massif du Mont Blanc

Most of the great mountains which make up le Massif du Mont Blanc, the highest part of the Alps, are situated in France. The frontier with Italy is oriented southwest by northeast; from Mont Dolent, the Franco-Swiss border is oriented in a northerly direction. In both instances, the borders pass through a succession of landmark ridges on which many famous peaks can be found. These range from Mont Blanc to Dent du Géant and Grandes Jorasses, and include Les Droites, Mont Maudit, Aiguilles du Midi, and countless others.

At the center of le Massif du Mont Blanc lies the celebrated Mer de Glace, second largest glacier in the Alps, which adds to the beauty and appeal of this incomparable region.

1. Mont Blanc, *4,807 m*

On several occasions I passed through the Mont Blanc tunnel to get into Italy, leaving behind the clear skies of Chamonix. To my disappointment, each time the southern slope of the mountain was either snowy or misty. Such bad weather conditions were not favorable to photography. However, on my fourth try I was lucky; for the first time the sky in Italy was beautifully clear.

Near the sleeping village of Entrèves, I found a suitable overlook made of piled-up hard-frozen snow. I waited there for sunrise, setting up my cameras. Soon, the morning light broke on Mont Blanc's summit. Within minutes sunshine had covered the steep slope, brightening the snow and rocks. A high cloud at the summit, called "Mont Blanc's Donkey"– usually an unwelcome indication that bad weather is coming–reflected the light and turned it into beautiful colors. It was a wonderful feast for the eyes.

2. Mont Blanc, *4,807 m*

From La Palud, a mountain village with an elevation of 1,370 meters on the Italian side of le Massif du Mont Blanc, I went to Refuge Torino (3,371 m). Usually, it is better to go up to Pointe Helbronner (3,462 m) than to Refuge Torino to get pictures of Mont Blanc and Aiguille Verte.

Over the V-shaped valley into which Mer de Glace descends, the famous Dent du Midi could be seen in the distance, and Aiguilles de Chamonix on the left looked beautiful to me. I was overwhelmed by Mont Blanc that day towards the end of summer, as the massive peak stood out in strong contrast to the clouds which had sprung up from Val Veni.

3. Mont Blanc de Courmayeur, *4,748 m*

Courmayeur, situated on the Italian side of le Massif du Mont Blanc, is a restful town similar to Chamonix. The cable car station at the center of town was crowded with people on vacation. When our party of four rode up to Youla, in the process transferring cars twice, our camera equipment took up as much space as two men, making the cabin crowded. At the height of 2,626 meters, bivouacking was naturally cold, but starry skies compensated for this. The next morning was splendid. The top of Mont Blanc was hidden by Mont Blanc de Courmayeur, which is almost the same height. The view had a rugged appearance different from what I had seen previously.

4. Pointe de l'Innominata, *3,730 m,* Aiguille Croux, *3,251 m*

At the southern slope of Mont Blanc, the gigantic ridge lying between Glacier de Freiney and Glacier de Brouillard reaches up to Mont Blanc de Courmayeur. Only Youla in Italy is a better spot for the frontal view of this ridge, which includes Aiguille Croux, Pointe de l'Innominata, and Arête de l'Innominata. That day, Mont Blanc was veiled by thick mist. A few hours later, the top of Courmayeur appeared occasionally. The sun shone strongly in the west, and Mont Blanc seemed more solid as shadows deepened along the spine ridges and in the deeply gouged-out valleys. The close-up of Pointe de l'Innominata and Aiguille Croux embossed by the light was exactly what I wanted to photograph.

5. Aiguille Noire, *3,773 m,* Aiguille Blanche, *4,108 m*

Another gigantic ridge lying between Glacier de Freiney and Glacier de la Brenva, which is located to the east of l'Innominata's ridge, is called Arête de Peuterey. Located beneath it is the beautiful, triangular Aiguille Noire de Peuterey. Above it rises the massive Aiguille Blanche de Peuterey. This arête includes Dames Anglaises, Pointe Gugliermina and other peaks. Surrounding this arête are numerous climbing routes, including the southwest wall of Pointe Gugliermina and Grand Pilier d'Angle de Peuterey, the north wall of Peuterey. Aiguille Noire and Aiguille Blanche in the setting sun, as seen from Youla, made me see a new aspect of the Alps.

6. Mont Blanc, *4,807 m*

Last night at Refuge Torino, and tonight at Aiguille du Midi, I stayed at heights of more than 3,000 meters. Tonight it was necessary to bivouac in a cable hut at an altitude of 3,795 meters. The only way to take good pictures of le Massif du Mont Blanc's morning and evening appearance from Aiguille du Midi is by bivouacking.

In the morning, a sea of clouds covered the valley of Arve up to Genève, and the town of Chamonix was completely hidden. The sky above was blue and clear, and a strong wind was blowing. Clouds in the west worried me, but, as it turned out, the weather was less of a problem than I had feared it might be. The sunset glow began on three mountains: Aiguille Verte, Les Droites, and Les Courtes. The hard wind blew in noisy gusts, and the overlook trembled like a leaf. During the shot I worried about the trembling.

7. Mont Blanc du Tacul, *4,258 m*

From the frozen slopes of Aiguille du Midi, we descended through Vallée Blanche on skis. Though not a difficult slope technically, the course is a long one, curving from Aiguille du Midi to Chamonix over a thirty-kilometer distance. I had long thought about skiing this slope, and in the middle of March, when the job of taking photos was almost over, I had the chance to do it. We didn't dare to carry much in the way of equipment, only what was necessary. Even so, our party of five men had a heavy load. Looking up at the mountains from the bottom of this white valley made us forget our burdens. Mont Blanc du Tacul, unimpressive when viewed from Aiguille du Midi, now stood out against the sky, massive and close to us. Thin clouds did not prevent us from capturing the mountain on film.

8. Mont Maudit, *4,463 m*

Mont Maudit is joined to Mont Blanc by a ridge stretching to the northeast. If you look further in this direction, you will find Mont Blanc du Tacul standing out. The view from Aiguille du Midi makes us think that it is only a peak, because the arête disappears in Vallée Blanche. Actually, this mountain stands out imposingly from Col Maudit.

    The best views of this mountain can be taken from Helbronner on the Italian side. The time of day best suited to photographing Mont Maudit is either morning or afternoon. To be more precise, it is when the morning sun glows and the afternoon sun brings out the textures of the rocks that good results can be obtained, when the climb has been made from Refuge Torino to Helbronner. That morning I was pleased with the view from Helbronner.

9. Mont Blanc, *4,807 m*

The weather was terrible, and we had to waste a few days without much significant activity. The north wind that began to blow that morning was the helping hand of God. We hurriedly climbed Aiguille du Midi, but the wild weather kept us from seeing anything. Hours spent waiting at the windy overlook were as difficult as those days we had spent doing nothing. This time, our efforts were rewarded. The wind tore through Vallée Blanche, and Mont Blanc emerged from the swirling fog. This was a new view of Mont Blanc, which usually stands out clearly against the blue sky. The fog made Mont Blanc appear to be the King of the Alps.

10. Aiguille Noire, *3,773 m*

Seven years ago, I first noticed this aiguille. At that time, I had just finished dining in Entrèves. I boarded a cable car, and as I looked through the window of the steeply ascending car, I suddenly caught sight of an aiguille which seemed to reach for the sky. Dark and gray-colored, the aiguille was vividly outlined against the backlight of the brightly shining sky.

    After that first experience, I visited Aiguille Noire several times, but I could never encounter the conditions which had created my first impression. On this winter morning Aiguille Noire was covered with snow, and I quivered with keen anticipation.

11. Aiguille Noire, *3,773 m*

Helbronner may be the main overlook for Aiguille Noire, but the view it provides is limited to the outline of the east ridge which stretches out from Col de Peuterey. From Lac du Miage in Val Véni one can view the west face as well as the south ridge above Glacier de Peuterey. This view doesn't correspond to my image of the aiguille, however. The view from Entrèves did not satisfy me fully, nor did that from le Pré de Pascal, which is a bit higher in elevation. The last place I visited was Lac du Chécroui. This hill was reached by cable car from Courmayeur, and gave me a perfect view of Aiguille Noire in the mist. At last I felt satisfied.

12. Gran Paradis, *4,061 m*

Aiguille du Midi commands a 360 degree view and has three overlooks. One is on the top of a ridge (3,795 m), another is on the top of the mountain (3,842 m), and the third is close by the second, to the west. They are close together, but there are subtle differences between them. It is hard to tell which vantage point is best. The view from the top of the mountain seems to me a bit better than the others. Usually I spent a whole day at this overlook. Bad weather had been hanging over the Alps, but this winter day seemed more stable. I watched the mountains from afar, without feeling the wind or the cold, separated from them by Vallée Blanche and Val d'Aosta.

13. Aiguille de Bionnassay, *4,051 m*

Aiguille de Bionnassay is located in front of Dôme du Goûter, where the ridge descending toward the northwest from Mont Blanc curves westward. Seen from a distance, this aiguille seems to be merely a shoulder of Mont Blanc; a slight change in viewing angle reveals it as a beautiful, independent peak. The north-south wall that dives into Glacier de Bionnassay at the altitude of 1,000 meters is especially fascinating, its climbing route covered with ice and rocks. Since there were not many fine days in that season, I was really busy during the few days in March when the weather was wonderful.

14. Aiguilles de Chamonix

Aiguilles de Chamonix begins with Aiguille du Midi (3,842 m) and extends towards the northeast, encompassing Aiguille du Plan, Aiguille de Blaitière, Aiguille du Grépon, Aiguilles des Grands Charmoz, Aiguille de la République, and Aiguille de l'M. In addition, such summits as Aiguille du Peigne, Aiguille des Pelerins, Aiguille du Fou, Dent du Crocodile, Aiguille de Ciseaux, Pain du Sucre, and Dent du Requin stand side by side. They provided us with superb climbing routes. The sunset glowing on Aiguilles de Chamonix, as seen from the town of Chamonix, can only be described with the word "grandeur."

15. Aiguilles du Midi, *3,842 m,* Eperon des Cosmiques, *3,842 m*

Cosmiques is adjacent to the south-southwest wall of Aiguille du Midi, and can actually be considered a part of the south wall. As an object of rock climbing, it is slightly easier than the south wall of Aiguille du Midi. I was pleased with myself when I skied the snowfield of Vallée Blanche. Cosmique rose above the snowfield, its yellow rocks bright against the blue sky. The grand granite mass seemed to represent the poetry of nature. The drama of that setting heightened my desire to take pictures.

16. Aiguilles du Midi, *3,842 m*

The south wall of Aiguille du Midi rises eighty meters higher than Cosmiques, and is judged a difficult climb. The first ascent was accomplished by Maurice Baquet and Gaston Rebuffat in July 1956. Unlike the summit of Midi, which can be ascended easily by cable from Chamonix, the south wall is still the place where a man challenges nature with his own hands and legs, and must employ the best climbing techniques. In summer, we saw such a challenge from the window of a cable car connecting Aiguilles du Midi and Helbronner. In winter, nobody was seen on this south wall. Then that yellowish aiguille rising from the snowfield resembled a vicious devil's fang.

17. Aiguilles de Chamonix

On the right-hand side of the Arve river, in the valley of Chamonix, some aiguilles stand face to face with Aiguilles du Midi. They are collectively named le Massif d'Aiguilles Rouges and consist of such aiguilles as Le Brévent, Pointe Clochers-Clocheton, Aiguille du Pouce, Aiguilles de la Glière, Aiguille du Belvédère, Aiguille de la Persévérance, and La Flégère. Some of them are located beneath eastern Ludex, and a ropeway is laid down from Les Praz to there. Both La Flégère and Lac Blanc are located further to the northeast and are known as splendid overlooks for Aiguilles de Chamonix. The view never grows dull, as it includes Grandes Jorasses at the back of Mer de Glace, Aiguille Berte and Aiguille du Dru. Aiguilles de Chamonix is so filled with beauty, especially in the afternoon light, that a camera can never catch its transformation fully.

18. Aiguilles de Chamonix

Refuge du Couvercle is located at an ideal spot in le Massif du Mont Blanc. To begin with, you can get a satisfactory view of the north wall of Grandes Jorasses from there. You can spend a whole day relaxing there, while comfortably viewing the mountains. During the day you can view Mont Blanc, Aiguilles de Chamonix, Mer de Glace's stripe lines, Les Droites, Les Courtes, and Aiguille du Triolet.

The Mountains of the Aiguilles de Chamonix seen from this spot are Dent du Requin, Aiguille du Plan, Dent du Crocodile, Dent du Caiman, Aiguille du Fou, Aiguille de Blaitière, Aiguille des Grands Charmoz. The view from this area differs from the view one gets from Chamonix.

19. Grand Charmoz, *3,444 m,* Dent du Requin, *3,422 m*

Descending from Le Montenvers to Mer de Glace, I became fatigued from crossing over the yawning crevasses and the streams flowing underneath the icefields. Our six-man party was heading for Refuge du Couvercle to shoot photos of Grandes Jorasses. Since we departed late, when we got to Glacier de Leschaux the sun was about to set in the west. When the sun touched on the ridge of Grands Charmoz the scenery around there was suddenly transformed. Dent du Requin dimmed in the backlight, then dissappeared. The sight of the wilderness called ''Fang of the Wolf'' revived my desire to shoot photos.

20. Aiguille de Blaitière, *3,522 m,* Aiguille du Grépon *3,482 m*

Afternoon is the best time for viewing Aiguilles de Chamonix from Pointe Helbronner. The effect of solidity, made by shadows when the afternoon light reaches to the south wall of the aiguilles, is far stronger than the views from Chamonix and Couvercle. My method is to stay at one spot, taking photos according to the changes of light in a day. This method affords me the ability to capture the changing appearance of the mountains from morning to evening. When the weather is stable, I can leisurely photograph mountains as I like to. This photo is a case in point. The two days' photo-taking was relaxing and joyful with the exception of busy times morning and evening.

21. Glacier du Talèfre

The mountains surrounding Glacier du Talèfre begin with Aiguille du Moine, which is almost in the center of le Massif du Mont Blanc, located at the right hand side of Mer de Glace. The mountains then extend to the three mountains of Droites: Aiguille Verte, Les Droites, and Les Courtes, and then reach to Aiguille Ravanel, Aiguille Mummery, and Aiguille du Triolet. They stretch further from Point Isabella, through Aiguille Savoie, and end at Aiguilles de Pierre Joseph, which extends westward from Aiguille du Talèfre. An oval-shaped glacier flows into Mer de Glace. As it exits it is narrowed down by ridges making the shape of the glacier like a purse.

Aiguille du Midi provides an interesting view of the striped lines of Glacier du Talèfre during the summer and the autumn. From winter until spring, the glacier is a flat, whitish snowfield.

22. Mer de Glace

Mer de Glace, meaning ''the sea of ice,'' is the second largest and longest glacier in the Alps, exceeded only by the Grosser Aletschgletscher in Berner Oberland. The sources of Mer de Glace are in Vallée Blanche, Glacier du Géant and Périades. They stream into Glacier du Tacul. Glacier de Leschaux, which combines with Glacier du Géant and Glacier du Mont Mallet, then flows into Glacier du Tacul. The combination of these glaciers is called Mer de Glace.

Grosser Aletschgletscher has beautiful vertical lines made by moraines. The chief characteristic of Mer de Glace is the growth ring of the glacier, which appears as crescent shapes on the ice at certain intervals. In an aerial view, this is quite evident. The glacier descending from Le Montenvers doesn't have any growth rings but has innumerable crevasses.

23. Glacier des Bossons

Many glaciers lie dormant around Mont Blanc and only three, Glaciers des Bossons, de Taconnaz and de Bionnassay, are really moving. They flow down from a height of 4,807 meters at the top to about 1,400 meters within a distance of only 7.5 kilometers. Crevasses at the lower reaches of the glaciers offer formidable photographic prospects. These glaciers don't flow among the mountains, and unlike Mer de Glace or Glacier d'Argentière they can be seen from Chamonix. Moreover, several minutes' climbing from Les Bossons takes you near the tip of the huge mass of moving ice. But, after all, the top of the Brévent gives you the best scene, for here it is that the Glacier des Bossons plunges into the Chamonix valley from the peak of Mont Blanc.

24. Glacier des Bossons, Chaine des Aravis

The Chamonix valley was veiled over by thick clouds, but le Massif de Mont Blanc rose above them. Occasionally cloudlets and vapor trails hid the sun, but they were soon blown away by high winds. It was unusually cold for early March, and I always had to wait at the Midi overlook for the best light to photograph. This usually made me apprehensive. At last, Glacier des Bossons, which had appeared just a mass of white, came to assume a visible shape. The shadow of a ridge helped brighten the glacier. No sooner had I begun to focus my camera than I fell into the supreme happiness of being with the mountains, forgetting the cold and the time completely.

25. Dent du Géant, *4,013 m,* Aiguille de Rochefort, *4,001 m*

If you look northeastward from Pointe Helbronner, you can capture the sight of Dent du Géant protruding like a horn. The distance between them looks short. Actually, however, as the crow flies it is 2.5 kilometers, and if you walk, it naturally becomes longer. Its altitude from Col du Géant through Col de Rochefort to the top is about 650 meters, and grade three rock-climbing training is required to scale the rock face. Rochefort mountains and hills lie between Dent du Géant and Aiguille de Rochefort. They form a knife-like ridge covered with snow. As usual, I tried to take photos at sunset, to capture its changing appearance. I went on until only the tip of Géant and Rochefort reflected the setting sun's rays.

26. Glacier de Leschaux, Grandes Jorasses, *4,208 m*

The north face of Grandes Jorasses is one of the so-called three north faces of the Alps. The other two north faces are those of the Eiger and the Matterhorn. Grandes Jorasses is nicknamed Éperon Walker. The wall, 1,500 meters wide and 1,200 meters high, is regarded as the most beautiful and the most difficult to scale among the north faces. Refuge de Couvercle is the most appropriate viewing place; from here you can enjoy its magnificent image. Grandes Jorasses has six points, all over 4,000 meters high. The highest is Pointe Walker, followed by Pointes Whymper, Croz, Hélène, and Marguerite. A four-member party from Japan scaled the central corridor in March 1972 for the first time. The party members were Yasuo Kato, Toru Nakano, Yasuo Kanda and Kazuhide Saito.

27. Grandes Jorasses, *4,208 m*

Grandes Jorasses is an interesting mountain. It presents an attractive view from any direction. If the superior sight from Refuge de Couvercle is excluded, the views from Lac Blanc, La Flégère and Midi as well as several places in Italy never mar the impression of Grandes Jorasses; rather to our surprise we always find new charms. For this reason, it is a fascinating mountain. The prospect from Midi is literally a profile. It reveals how steep the north face is. Whenever I look at the scene, I can't help taking pictures, for the mountain rising up into the firmament is most attractive to me. Unfortunately we must wait a long time for good photographic opportunities, because Grandes Jorasses seldom gets the sun.

28. Mer de Glace, Grandes Jorasses, *4,208 m*

A wonderful blue sky lasted briefly and then clouds crept over the descent of Vallée Blanche. By the time we finished lunch at Refuge de Requin, the sky was veiled completely by the clouds. We decided it was impossible to take more photographs, and after a long rest, we began our descent at about 4:00 P.M. Though it was a gentle slope, we were forced to ski at a tremendous speed because the snow had started to crust. Near Le Montenvers, where the glacier makes a great bend, the snow had thawed during a spell of bright days, and a section of upheaved ice was exposed. Ironically, however, bad weather at this juncture was in perfect accord with the intended image which I wished to communicate.

29. Grandes Jorasses, *4,208 m*

We passed Mer de Glace and entered the area of Glacier de Leschaux. At this side of its junction with the Glacier de Talèfre, we climbed a ladder put up at the right bank. It was almost vertical, and just like that of a firetower, it was made of thin metal. It was a long steep climb and there were several sections to the ladder. Furthermore we were loaded with heavy baggage and we nearly slipped off the ladder. Even after we had managed to climb the ladder we still had to ascend more than 350 meters to reach Refuge de Couvercle. Although it was late and drawing toward sunset, I was determined to take pictures there, for I could see the whole north face of Grandes Jorasses. It was past eight in the evening when I returned to the refuge after the photographing session.

30. Grandes Jorasses, *4,208 m*

I was always thinking of photographing Grandes Jorasses at dawn and dusk from the Aiguilles du Midi. One way or another, I wanted to take these photos, but Midi was not designed to meet my wish, since it lacked accommodations such as those found at Refuge Torino. At last my wish was realized, thanks to my friend Toru Nakano, who lives in Chamonix. I was able to stay at a cable station, because he was on nodding terms with local residents and guides. I had to take food and bedding there by myself. I started my picture-taking trip after trying to make certain that the weather was fine, although, as always, we had to take the weather as it came. Fortunately, the small hours of the morning found le Massif du Mont Blanc lying in clear and quiet weather. When the sun came up it illuminated the north wall of Grandes Jorasses.

31. Aiguille du Dru, *3,754 m,* Aiguille Verte, *4,122 m*

Whether or not I succeed in my work depends on luck. Sometimes I encounter favorable conditions easily. At other times, I try many times in vain. If I am lucky enough to meet fine weather on one visit, I'm sure to try my luck again. If I'm having bad luck, I obstinately go there over and over. It is truly a strange job.

I had good luck taking this picture of Aiguilles Dru and Verte. It had been rainy or cloudy for five days. On the day I climbed up to La Flégère, I moved quickly, although it was still cloudy; there were signs that good weather might arrive in the afternoon. My expectations were fulfilled. The good weather held until the next morning, but after that the weather turned bad and stayed that way. I was really lucky to have caught the brief interval of good weather.

32. Aiguille Verte, *4,122 m,* Les Droites, *4,000 m*

It had been raining for two days. On the morning of the third day, weather indications seemed to improve. Even though the outline of the mountains against the sky couldn't be seen, when the wind blew hard I was sure that the weather would clear. Because of cable car congestion, it was almost 10:00 A.M. when I arrived at Midi. I waited for almost two hours. As I had hoped, the mountains began to appear through the dissipating fog. The west wall of the Aiguille du Plan, usually too steep to be crowned with snow, was decorated with white rime that day. However, Aiguille Verte and Les Droites were even more splendid. My eyes and camera focused on Glacier de la Charpous, which had eaten its way into Aiguille Verte like a gigantic letter "Y." Arête Sans Nom and the long rock ridgeline adjacent to Aiguille du Moine completed the panorama.

33. Petit Dru, *3,733 m,* Grand Dru, *3,754 m*

The north face of Petit Dru is very famous, its reputation colored by a number of episodes which partake of history and legend. On the outskirts of Chamonix there is a campsite perfect for viewing Petit Dru. To reach it, one walks along the Arve River from Chamonix and Les Praz. From here, the west face of Petit Dru is visible. The vertical wall 1,000 meters high will astound you. However, I prefer the appearance of the thickset north face without knowing why. Also near the Arve is the short and thick peak Aiguilles des Grands Montets, near Argentière.

34. Aiguille Verte, *4,122 m,* Aiguille du Dru, *3,754 m*

Late in September, the cable cars to La Flégère stop running, so you must climb to Lac Blanc by yourself. From there you will have a wonderful view of Mont Blanc. I started at Argentière and reached Lac Blanc after a two and one half hours' walk. The quiet and loneliness of autumn was in the air; the busy summer was over. As I had expected, the cottage keeper was to descend the mountain that day. Therefore, we would have to camp in the tent village, since camping was now prohibited at the site where we had enjoyed viewing Aiguille Verte and Aiguilles de Chamonix.

35. Aiguille Verte, *4,122 m,* Les Droites, *4,000 m,*
Les Courtes, *3,856 m*

The Droites mountains include Aiguille Verte, Les Droites and Les Courtes. Verte is the highest and most famous; I always wondered why it is not called the three mountains of Verte. However, on a second look, I understood. Les Droites is the most magnificent in form among them. The other two are less imposing. I had arrived at Refuge de Argentière at around nine the previous night. André Contamine and Hitoshi Kondo, who arrived earlier, worried about me, since I was late. They proceeded to the northeast face, and when I arrived I gazed at the glorious alpenglow of Droites' three mountains.

36. Les Droites, *4,000 m*

If you want a better view of Les Droites' north face, you might climb a little higher than Refuge de Argentière at 2,771 meters. This place is too low, and Aiguille Argentière is too high to obtain the best view of the north face. I levelled the camera at the wall at about the 3,211 meter level. I had scaled Aiguille Argentière in 1955 for the first time. This cold and indifferent mountain has never allowed climbers to approach easily. Snow and ice cover the whole wall, and Droites will probably remain ''the north wall of north walls'' of the Alps forever. A winter climbing by way of the Jean Couzy route was made by my friends Masaru Suzuki and Toru Nakano in 1973.

37. Aiguille de Triolet, *3,870 m*

Aiguille de Triolet, with neighboring Mont Dolent on the border of Switzerland and Italy, lies deep in the area of Mont Blanc. The easiest way to climb this mountain is first to stop over at Refuge de Couvercle and then go to the Glacier de Talèfre. The best route for scaling the north face, equivalent to that of Grandes Jorasses in beauty, is to ascend Glacier d'Argentière. Triolet's north wall—800 meters high with 53 steep grades—ranks first in climbing difficulty. I waited to capture its cold and bleak impression. But the sun never shed its light. I became so irritated that I accidently released the shutter.

38. Glacier d'Argentière, Mont Dolent, *3,821 m*

The route to Refuge d'Argentière, a base for Mont Dolent in France, is to go up Aiguille des Grands Montets by ropeway from the Argentière village, and down Glacier des Rognons, then onto Glacier d'Argentière. Those who don't like this route get down at Rognons station, traverse and enter Glacier d'Argentière. You can get a distant view of Mont Dolent as it soars above the stretch of Glacier d'Argentière. Here the ancient quiet remains, for all artificial elements are eliminated. This place is surrounded by the ridge of Pointe de Domino which connects Verte, Les Droites and Les Courtes with Triolet and Mont Dolent.

39. Aiguille d'Argentière, *3,900 m,* Tour Noir, *3,837 m*

Confronting one another with Glacier d'Argentière between them are Droites' three mountains, and Aiguille du Chardonnet, Aiguille d'Argentière, Tour Noir and other mountains. As compared with the Droites on the left, the mountains on the right are lower in altitude but seem more beautiful. Grands Montets is the best overlook for this range. It was just before sunset that the ridges seemed most beautiful. A flaming sunset tinged the rocks of the mountains with a rosy flush.

40. Aiguille du Chardonnet, *3,824 m*

It had taken too much time to photograph Grands Montets. It was 4:00 P.M. when I started descending Glacier des Rognons. We had a summer snow of more than twenty centimeters the previous day and the thaw made it easy to ski. I found myself approaching Aiguille du Chardonnet gradually. "I want to take a picture of this beauty, but I must return to Refuge d'Argentière before sunset," I thought to myself, since my friends were waiting for me. I had some inner conflict but since I gave priority to my work, I apologized to my friends in a corner of my heart and I began photographing. As a result, I captured a lurid and gorgeous sunset no one else has ever seen. My heart beat rapidly with delight, as I went down the glacier in the darkness.

Wallis (Valais)

If the Wallis Alps leave to le Massif du Mont Blanc the supremacy of altitude, for themselves they claim title to a large area in which numerous peaks over 4,000 meters can be found. From Simplon up to the Franco-Swiss frontier over a hundred kilometers in this range are filled with valleys, including d'Herens, Saastal, Matterthal, and d'Anniviers. The range is bordered in the south by Val d'Aoste. Along the Italian border rise the summits of Grand St. Bernard, Monte Rosa, and of course, the famous Matterhorn, called Cervino in Italian.

41. Monte Rosa, *4,634 m,* Liskamm, *4,527 m*

Monte Rosa, the second highest peak in the Alps, has a rather stumpy shape in comparison to the sharp appearance of the Matterhorn, located just opposite. We get a false impression of bluntness and heaviness, especially because Gornergrat limits our view, and also because the angle from which we view Monte Rosa makes a difference. Neighboring Liskamm is also wide, but luckily we can see its height more clearly, and this helps to give it a neat image. We had enjoyed a full day just looking at Monte Rosa and Liskamm; now, these mountains were covered with twilight which bathed their numerous peaks—each one over 4,000 meters high—in a golden glow.

42. Monte Rosa, *4,634 m*

Changing cable cars twice, we reached Schwarzsee (2,583 m) from Zermatt. We were directly below the Matterhorn; across the valley of Gornergletscher we could see Monte Rosa. From Schwarzsee, Monte Rosa looks much the way it did when we viewed it from Gornergrat. Actually, Monte Rosa is so huge and grand that slight changes in viewing angles made little or no difference. The wind blew so hard that clouds were constantly being created and driven away. The next day's weather was still less certain, so we took photographs despite the possibility that the wind might blur and blunt our efforts.

43. Monte Rosa, *4,634 m*

It is foolish to be anxious about the weather today or tomorrow in my profession. Sometimes we simply have to wait patiently for a glimpse of clear sky, all the while exposed to chilly winds. When the sky clears, however briefly, we experience our most thrilling moments. In this case, I had spent five nights in Gornergrat waiting for the right opportunity; next I went from the valley of d'Arolla by car to Täsch; from there, I took the railway to Zermatt. The train and hotel were almost deserted, except for our party. But the loneliness was minor, and this photograph brightened my heart. Right after the picture was taken, the mountain sank beneath thick clouds.

44. Castor, *4,228 m*, Pollux, *4,092 m*

On the fifth day of our stay in Gornergrat, fine weather finally arrived. I was busy taking photos, and had begun to think of reloading the camera with film. Just at that moment I noticed some peaks that seemed to be floating in sea-beds. The shaded parts looked pale blue, almost like the color of the ocean. These peaks were Zwillinge, the twin mountains (Castor and Pollux). On this day I discovered that even ordinary mountains can become ideal models under the right conditions.

45. Breithorn, *4,165 m*

The name Breithorn means "broad mountain." There is another peak in Berner Oberland with the same name, but I prefer this one, which is so big that I have always had to hesitate a moment, as I try to plan the composition of the photograph. Breithorn is 2.5 kilometers high at its summit, and it includes a range of seven peaks, all over 4,000 meters high. Although it is not easy to photograph this mountain, we used its broad base to express grandeur, and created three-dimensional and cubic effects with a careful use of light and shadow.

46. Breithorn, *4,165 m*

The weather was improving gradually, and the clouds over Monte Rosa and Liskamm were driven away; soon I would be able to view the clear, snow-covered surface of Breithorn. My long-awaited view of the Matterhorn darkened as usual. Surrounding peaks were visible, but the Matterhorn was lost beneath clouds. Because it stands alone, the Matterhorn is easily veiled by clouds, even on clear days. I sat waiting for a chance to catch a view of the summit. Suddenly, a bright ray of sunlight penetrated to Gornergletscher, and, climbing to the middle of Breithorn, revealed a dim peak line. I moved my fingers without thinking, snapping the photograph.

47. Matterhorn, *4,478 m*

No one will oppose naming the Matterhorn the chief of the Wallis mountains. If you compare them in altitude only, the Matterhorn is ranked fourth in the Wallis range, which has such giants as Monte Rosa, second highest in the whole Alps, Liskamm (4,527 m), and Weisshorn (4,505 m). Even Dom and Täschhorn in the Mischabel range just next to Wallis are higher than the Matterhorn.

Then why is the Matterhorn the leader? There are several reasons. It is the only one visible from Zermatt; it is an independent mountain undisturbed by others; and among all others its matchless beauty is enough to appoint it as the chief. People have always praised its balanced, glacier-scraped figure. This picture was taken at Lake Grindji.

48. Matterhorn, *4,478 m*

The following are just several famous spots from which to take pictures of the beautiful Matterhorn: Zermatt, Winkelmatter, Findeln, Riffelalp. And we can also name Gornergrat, Riffelsee, Schwarzsee and so on. Because the Matterhorn stands alone among the Alps and can be easily seen in many places, it is also difficult to shoot the superb figure properly. On this trip, soon after we finished working in Gornergrat, we proceeded to Schwarzsee. The wind was blowing wildly causing a snowstorm, and the Matterhorn was covered with clouds which were reflecting fiery colors from the sun which was hidden behind them. I remembered that the Matterhorn has a fate described as ''glorious and tragic.''

49. Matterhorn, *4,478 m*

An eastern wall composed of the Hornligrat on the right and the Furggrat on the left contributes to the Matterhorn's beauty as it stretches upward toward the sky. This scene is of an angle taken from Gornergrat to Gornergletscher; a view from Riffelberg toward Zermatt will give us a different impression with Zmuttgrat on the right. I've been busy in Gornergrat. I could have concentrated on the Matterhorn if there had been only the Matterhorn, but there are four other peaks between Weisshorn and Dent Blanche which were shining red and they kept me busy photographing them. I can never overlook scorching rocks towering in the sky.

50. Matterhorn, *4,478 m*

By climbing down from Gornergrat to Zermatt, we come to Rotenboden; a little further on there is a small lake called Riffelsee, famous for its reflection of the Matterhorn. The lake would be ice-covered by now. I continued to climb down and reached Riffelberg, where we could see different views of the Matterhorn from Zmuttgrat to the right of Hornligrat. Photographers appreciate Riffelberg more than Gornergrat, as a site for viewing the Matterhorn. I was deeply absorbed in watching the clouds at the top of the Matterhorn, and I took many photos.

51. Matterhorn, *4,478 m*

We spent a full day in the area from Gornergrat to Riffelalp. Though surrounding mountains are included in pictures of Rotenboden, the Matterhorn stands alone after Riffelberg is passed. The weather was stable and the season was right, as it was the middle of the summer, and we enjoyed a perfect mountain stroll. Walking down from Riffelalp, we entered the village of Findeln, famous for its chocolates. The view of the Zmuttgrat range with the afternoon light penetrating sharply and shining on the northern wall of the Matterhorn brought this summer's wonderful trip to a climactic finish for us.

52. Monte Cervino (Matterhorn), *4,478 m*

Leonegrat of the Matterhorn can not be viewed from Switzerland. In Italy, to see the Matterhorn, which is called Monte Cervino there, you have to come to Valtournanche through the valley of Aosta. There is Cervinia (Breuil) famous for its ski base at the end of the valley. I visited Testa Grigia (Plateau Rosa) three times. The smog which wholly covered the white surroundings was suddenly cleared when evening came. I could see the violent-tempered Monte Cervino climbing towards the sky from a low altitude of 2,000 meters; the mountain stood out, greatly contrasted against the clouds. I felt that I had seen a new face of Monte Cervino shining in the twilight.

53. Dom, *4,545 m,* Täschhorn, *4,491 m*

The Mischabel mountains are hardly known to people, although they are part of the Wallis group geographically. The mountains along the rivers in Mattervispa are represented by the Matterhorn and a few other peaks such as Monte Rosa, Liskamm, and Breithorn which have their own fame. Weisshorn, Zinalrothorn and Ober Gabelhorn are less acknowledged, and the least known category includes Dent Blanche and Dent d'Hérens located in the dead end of a valley. The Mischabels are also unfortunate in that Dom and Täschhorn, which are higher than the Matterhorn, seem to share in bearing the adversity of the Matterhorn's proximity. I feel the sharp peaks of these twin mountains are symbols of loneliness in Mischabel.

54. Dent Blanche, *4,357 m*

I am fond of this "White Fang." I remember in Jack London's *White Fang* that the hero of the novel had a stern and aloof character. I feel this character matches the mountain figure towering over the Schonbielgletscher at the end of the Mattervispa River. The best photos can be taken from Gornergrat, especially on summer mornings. It is necessary for the sun to be in the north so that it will bring out the contrast in the unevenness of the mountain surface. I still remember Dent Blanche in Val d'Arolla where it appeared to be just sitting over the village of Les Hauderes. Putting these good memories aside, the morning sun on this day instantly changed the "White Fang" to "Red Fang."

55. Dent Blanche, *4,357 m,* Ober Gabelhorn, *4,063 m*

Rotenboden is one station before Gornergrat, which is the terminal of the mountain railway originating in Zermatt. Getting off at Rotenboden, which few people will do, you walk into Gornergletscher, the location of the Riffelsee. As Riffelsee is normally noisy and crowded with hikers in the summer, my favorite season to visit there is autumn. I used to visit Riffelsee's lake-side from Gornergrat at daybreak, when there were no people around, and I could enjoy the beautiful relections of mountain ranges starting with Monte Rosa on the lake. At that hour all is quiet, which helps to separate reality from reflection. But only a few moments are allowed for me to enjoy the company of the mountains and the lake. Soon the calmness of the atmosphere is broken by hikers.

56. Ober Gabelhorn, *4,063 m*

With Zmuttgletscher between them, Ober Gabelhorn confronts the Matterhorn. Unter Gabelhorn at 3,391 meters stands in front of the mountain and blocks Ober Gabelhorn from Zermatt's view. It is said that Horace Walker, A. W. Moore, and a few others first succeeded in climbing to the top of Ober Gabelhorn in 1865, which coincides with the Matterhorn conquest by Whymper. I entered into the valley of Zinal to the west of Ober Gabelhorn, searching for new angles to view it, but did not succeed. Gornergrat seems to be the best place to photograph Ober Gabelhorn even though Unter Gabelhorn partially blocks it.

57. Zinalrothorn, *4,221 m*

Zinalrothorn is actually 160 meters higher than Ober Gabelhorn, although the two peaks beside each other give us the impression of twin mountains. The name "Zinalroth" is used because this mountain is located at the end of Zinalgletscher, source of the Zinal valley. Hohlichtgletscher is piped to the Mattervispa River. The glacier shown in the photo is Rothorngletscher, which joins Triftgletscher and reaches Zermatt. Though Zinalrothorn is considered part of the Zinal ranges, the image of the mountain is not so appealing when we see it on the Zinal side. I am planning to look for other ways to shoot Zinalrothorn on my next trip.

58. Weisshorn, *4,505 m*

Confronting the Mischabel mountains, Weisshorn–"white mountain"–is the highest of the ranges on the left bank of the Mattervispa River. Weisshorn has a perfectly three-cornered triangular shape, facing west, northeast and southwest, and thus it differs from the Matterhorn which is four-cornered. While I waited at the lower end of the Gornergrat sunbeams gradually illuminated the Weisshorn and started revealing the unique vertical line of it. I was sorry that a portion of the Matterhorn hindered showing the height of Weisshorn.

59. Weisshorn, *4,505 m*

At high altitudes in Europe, the sun rises quite early and sets late. The length of daytime is noticeable high in the mountains. A person like me, who has to stand by before dawn and continue to take photos even after sunset, will definitely lack sleep whenever fine weather continues for several days. Even so, if there is bad weather for several days during such a trip, I wish that an occasional fine day would stay longer, for such time flies by. A high wind during the afternoon was badly troubling the Matterhorn, and the mountains of Mischabel, and had begun affecting neighboring ranges. Light reflecting on the west face of Weisshorn was greatly magnified by the cloud cover near the mountain. This photo was taken in Schwarzsee.

60. Zermatt and Matterhorn, *4,478 m*

It was our second night in Zermatt. We had stayed six days in Gornergrat and five days in Schwarzsee. The past two weeks we'd had such bad weather that we were rather fed up. We decided to go outside when it stopped snowing in the evening. Crossing the tracks of mountain railways and the Mattervispa River, we took a walk to where we could have a bird's-eye view of Zermatt. This path, leading to the skiing course of Sunnegga, was crowded with skiers, and we had a tough time passing them. In setting the camera and waiting, the evening light gradually strengthened and was reflected on the newly fallen snow. As if replying to the beauty of the scene the snow-covered Matterhorn emerged in the twilight sky.

Berner Oberland

The Berner Oberland range is located in the Central Alps as is the Wallis range, and almost all of the mountains in this range are situated in Switzerland. There are world famous mountains in the Berner Oberland group such as Jungfrau, Mönch, and the Eiger, which is rated third for climbing difficulty. Jungfrau, the chief of the three, can be best viewed in the mountain town of Interlaken. Finsteraarhorn is the highest peak of Berner Oberland and surrounding it are such notables as Lauteraarhorn, Fiescherhorn, Schreckhorn, and Wetterhorn. On the west bank of Grosser Aletschgletscher are Aletschhorn, Breithorn and Blümlisalphorn.

61. Jungfrau, *4,158 m*

Jungfrau is the most famous mountain in the Berner Oberland range. Although Finsteraarhorn is higher, it is situated in the heart of the range, so that you must first travel from Grindelwald and then go up to Faulhorn to get a view of it. Since Finsteraarhorn is less appealing, it is natural that Jungfrau, nicely visible even at the foot of Kleine Scheidegg, is the more popular peak. Jungfrau is generally considered to be the chief peak in the locality. The viewing of Jungfrau is not without limits, however: it must be seen either from the north or the west, and the mountain is illuminated only in the afternoon.

62. Jungfrau, *4,158 m*

I was worried about the weather as I rode back to Interlaken. The weather had been miserable for the last eight days, and I went to Zurich only to purchase film. But I didn't know whether I would be able to use it. As I proceeded to Lauterbrunnen by car, and to Wengen and Kleine Scheidegg by railway, I was preoccupied with the changing weather. At last I could see Jungfrau over my head, reflecting a rosy color in the evening sunlight.

63. Jungfrau, *4,158 m*

Kleine Scheidegg is reached by mountain railway from Grindelwald or Lauterbrunnen. There we can get magnificent views of famous mountains: Wetterhorn and Breithorn. If we go up to Jungfraujoch by rail, we can see Jungfrau, Mönch, and Grosser Aletschgletscher. It is like standing on a lookout in heaven. Jungfrau as seen from Jungfraujoch has a rugged look; the view differs greatly from the one in Kleine Scheidegg and other lookout points. The east wall of Jungfrau extends to Grosser Aletschgletscher, and the sharp knife-ridge at the summit looks as if it is daring us to attack it for a climb.

64. Mönch, *4,099 m*

Seven years ago I first visited here. A thick fog had surrounded the mountains of Berner Oberland. It was drizzling on the following day when we left for a hike. Avoiding the crowded Grindelwald, we walked to Kleine Scheidegg. We were descending a gentle slope when it stopped raining and dim rays of sunlight started to show between the clouds, but we were unable to see either the Eiger or the Wetterhorn. Next day I took a trip to Jungfraujoch; I waited to photograph Mönch until dark on a hill near the hotel.

65. Eiger, *3,970 m*

First is reached from Grindelwald by connecting lifts and it is 2,168 meters high. It's famous for its lookout from which one can view Eiger, Fiescherhorn, Schreckhorn, and Wetterhorn. It was still April and the morning sun didn't reach the north wall of Eiger. Therefore, I climbed First to take photographs of the Eiger's afternoon and evening illumination. Spring had already come to Grindelwald, and small flowers could be spotted through the remaining patches of snow. The observation point was still wintry because of its high altitude; despite my wishes it began snowing wildly in the afternoon. I managed to get permission to spend the night in a cable hut, with neither sleeping bags nor other comforts. I was satisfied in that I was able to view the mountains from a good vantage point the next morning, although it was misty.

66. Eiger, *3,970 m,* Mönch, *4,099 m*

I visited the lookout several times to photograph Eiger in the evening glow. There are other observation spots, such as Kleine Scheidegg, Mürren, and Grutschalp. But I wasn't satisfied with any view of Eiger I could find, so I walked around eagerly searching for the right place, all the while worrying that I'd miss the sunset. I decided there is no better place than Kleine Scheidegg. I waited there patiently day after day, and finally caught the sunset. It began abruptly, when the evening sun reached halfway up the north wall of Eiger, and it soon disappeared.

67. Eiger, *3,970 m*

When we look up from Kleine Scheidegg at 2,161 meters, Eiger astonishes us with its steep north wall. In summer the Eiger's reddish rock wall contrasts sharply against the other mountains which are covered with a soft green hue. The stilled north wall seemed to be enjoying a moment of peace before it had to face the summer traffic. Climbers had challenged it with a strong determination to conquer it, but during its severe winter it's allowed to doze for a while. Soon summer will come and then the Eiger must be exposed to people's curious eyes. Soon the Eiger will be ready to battle the climbers again.

68. Wetterhorn, *3,701 m*

Going south from Interlaken, you turn to the right along Lauterbrunnen, a path at Zwei-lütschinen, and enter the valley of Schwarze Lütschine. The moment you see the village of Grindelwald, a mountain will emerge from the bottom of a gorge blocking the way. People who see it at first may doubt that it is a mountain, for it is made of a lump of rocks, but it is the Wetterhorn. The summit consists of three peaks, and they are Haslungfrau, normally called Wetterhorn, Mittelhorn at 3,704 meters, and Rosenhorn which is a little lower than the others. The north wall should be called the northwest wall to be more exact, and its top is Haslungfrau.

69. Wetterhorn, *3,701 m*

I had slept in my clothes in the cable hut, while the persistent snow was falling. The next morning I found it had all stopped and fresh snow lay twenty centimeters deep on the top of the older snow. Several stars twinkled in the dusky light and morning mist already swirled around First, which is 2,168 meters high. A dim sunrise was the gift for those who had spent the night here. There were no bright morning colors. As the fog increased in density it glittered like scaly powder. Though the grandeur of the mountain was lost, I took out a camera and set it in position to take pictures just as the sun became a stream of light through the fog.

70. Wetterhorn, *3,701 m*

The second day in Kleine Scheidegg began with the morning glow over the Wetterhorn. I didn't feel like taking pictures of it, for most of the Wetterhorn was veiled by darkness. I left for Jungfraujoch and came back that same afternoon; then I went to a point half way between Kleine Scheidegg and Eigergletscher and decided to have an outstaring game with Breithorn, Jungfrau, Mönch, Eiger and Wetterhorn. The length of the summer day cornered the sun far to the north. Shadows began to form on Wetterhorn, which had been dull in the flat sunlight. It was just past five o'clock and heavy clouds clung to the base of the mountain.

71. Schreckhorn, *4,078 m,* Lauteraarhorn, *4,042 m*

These mountains, both over 4,000 meters in height, can't be viewed frontally because their valley is deep and both peaks rise steeply. The mountains of Berner Oberland seem not to have progressed fully from the Ice Age. Whole ranges are in one big table plateau and the rock summit above it is a swollen glacier. Schreckhorn and Lauteraarhorn begin to reveal themselves when we come close to Oberhus, the first station from Grindelwald by lift. The crest-shaped peak becomes even clearer as the lift comes near First. It looks as if ''Yama,'' the Japanese character for mountain, has been written on the mountains when we see them together, with Schreckhorn in front and Lauteraarhorn in back.

72. Fiescherhorn, *4,049 m,* Fieschergletscher

Eiger is easily accessible from the valley of Zweilütschinen in Grindelwald, for vehicles are always available. Putting aside Wetterhorn which towers directly up from the bottom of the valley, we couldn't get close to Schreckhorn and Fiescherhorn. It became a question of being near Finsteraarhorn, highest of the group, because you must travel some distance by a long glacier to approach either from Fieschergletscher or the south Rhone valley. Fiescherhorn is difficult to reach but it is one of my favorite mountains. I am attracted to it because it reminds me of the South Alps of Japan, which I like best of all, although they differ in their surfaces, one being covered by snow and the other by trees.

73. Grosser Aletschgletscher, Aletschorn, *4,195 m*

Berner Oberland is called a "kingdom of snow and ice" and that name suits Grosser Aletschgletscher. Its total length is 26.8 kilometers and it is much longer than Mer de Glace, which ranks second. The source of the glacier is three peaks: Mönch, Jungfrau, and Aletschorn, whose small glaciers rise up to their respective summits. Ober Aletschgletscher is the largest branch and Mittel Aletschgletscher comes second. Though Grosser Aletschgletscher can be viewed in Jungfraujoch, the best lookout is Eggishorn, where you can see Aletschorn to the far left and Mönch and Jungfrau to the far right. Starting from Fiesch in the south Rhone, a cable car will take us to Eggishorn.

74. Breithorn, *3,785 m*

There are two Breithorns: one is in the Berner Oberland range and the other is in the Wallis mountains. This Breithorn is three meters shorter than the other, which is located one kilometer south-southwest, and its appearance is superior to the other. Leaving Lauterbrunnen for Largwald where the ropeway will take us to Gimmelwald, Mürren, and Birg, we finally arrive at the top of Schilthorn, 2,970 meters in height. Though the lookout at Schilthorn allows us to have bird's-eye views of Eiger, Mönch, Jungfrau, and Blümlisalp, I don't much care to watch any mountain except the Breithorn.

Alpi Bernina

This range is situated far to the east, but it is considered to be part of the Central Alps. Piz Bernina is the highest peak in Alpi Bernina with a height of 4,091 metters; it is the only one which measures over 4,000 meters. Other principal mountains are Piz Roseg, Piz Zupo, Piz Palu and Piz Morteratsch. Passing Passo del Maloja from Maloja, which is famous for paintings by the artist Giovanni Segantini, we enter Val Bregaglia. From there we are able to view Piz Cengalo and Piz Badile over Vadret da Bondasca. These mountains are made of granite and are worshipped by climbers. An important town in the valley of Oker Engadin is St. Moritz, known as a summer resort and skiing ground. It is surrounded by woods, lakes, and mountains.

75. Piz Palu, *3,905 m*

Piz Palu is a beautiful mountain. When I came across it the first time, I remembered Mt. Senjo of the South Alps in Japan. However, Mt. Senjo is 3,033 meters high and Piz Palu is 3,905 meters in height; Palu is covered with snow and rocks, while Mt. Senjo is protected by thick forest.

Three protruding peaks covered with rocks and ice are renowned as the north wall of Piz Palu, and there are great differences in altitude between the bottom of Vadret Pers and the top of the north wall respectively, so many climbers call here. To view Piz Palu, I recommend you go to Diavolezza, (2,973 m), then proceed by ropeway from north Val Bernina instead of approaching from the Engadin valley in St. Moritz. You will enjoy seeing brave Piz Palu across Vadret da Morteratsch right before your eyes.

76. Piz Palu, *3,905 m*

The more we want the morning weather to be fine during our stay at the mountain top, the more we feel worried about it. Consequently, if it turns out to be good weather our joy will be at its peak. We feel rather easy if there are broken clouds, or if few stars are twinkling when we look up at the night sky and on the contrary, our worries increase if it is fine with the sky full of stars for we have been deceived so often by the weather of the mountains that we have become skeptical. An unexpectedly fine morning has arrived on this occasion. As a little snow had been falling and some wind had been blowing on the previous night, I had little hope. When I woke to find that Piz Palu stood out against a blue sky, I was too pleased to go skiing.

77. Piz Zupo, *3,996 m*

Piz Zupo is a group of mountains in which there are eight peaks varying between 3,804 and 3,996 meters in height. Since the peaks are piled around its top just like Palu, it creates a rather dull impression. Whenever we take mountain pictures of this kind, we utilize the clouds whether we like them or not. And if there are no clouds, the slanting beams of the morning and evening sunlight will be utilized. Luckily at this time the clouds started forming in the midst of the morning beams. In this photograph, a crevasse is seen as a diagonal against the summit, which greatly contributes to the photo's success. Because of bad weather I had changed my itinerary and visited the demon mountain of Diavolezza several times before I was blessed with this opportunity.

78. Vadret da Monteratsch, Piz Zupo, *3,996 m*

Soon after we entered the Val Bernina from Celerina, northeast of St. Moritz, we came to a small town called Pontresina. Passing Pontresina, Piz Palu appears after a while on the left, and we come to Morteratsch, in which the end of Vadret da Monteratsch flows out from the principal mountains such as Piz Cambrena, Piz Palu, Piz Zupo, Piz Bernina and Piz Morteratsch. This is known also as the entrance to the hiking course to Diavolezza. The terrain here is unusual; glaciers of Alpi Bernina all terminate loosely. They normally form cliffs, but in this locality they flow in a steady slope and just end there.

79. Piz Bernina, *4,049 m*

I wonder how many times I have visited Piz Corvatsch (3,451 m) and Diavolezza. I have made repeated calls to both sites just to take photos of Piz Bernina, from the west and from the east respectively, but I have failed each time because of bad weather. In Diavolezza, which had accommodations, I became good friends with the military people who were staying there for training. They used to sympathize with me by saying, ''You haven't taken good pictures yet'' or ''Sorry for the unlucky day.'' But we were finally rewarded with very clear skies. The snow stopped falling and we congratulated each other while bathed in the reddish morning sunlight.

80. Piz Bernina, *4,049 m,* Piz Roseg, *3,931 m*

We started from a camping ground in St. Moritz heading for Fuorcla Surlej, the perfect lookout to view the west of Piz Bernina from the front. Since it was a fine day, the heavy load didn't bother us; and the October wind kept us comfortable. When we arrived in Cor a little past noon, Piz Bernina shone in the fall sunlight and Piz Roseg towered above Vadret da Tschierva, proudly showing its sharp peak. We found snow under a rock which had fallen a few days ago. Six of our party members enjoyed a nap, for the sun was still high and there was enough daylight left for taking photographs later. It was past seven o'clock when we returned to our tents.

81. Sciora, *3,215 m*

Passing Passo del Maloja, to the west from Vadret da Engadin, we entered Vadret da Bregaglia. Though it is located in Switzerland, it is perfectly Italian, as such village names as Vicosoprano and Promontogno indicate. We were sent to the village of Soglio, passing Promontogno where the path was paved with stones and we felt nostalgia for home. It is a simple mountain village with cottages made entirely of stone including the roofs, at a high altitude of 1,100 meters. It faces the Sciora mountains and Piz Badile. The Sciora range includes (from right to left) Sciora de Dentoro (3,275 m), Agodi (3,205 m), Pioda (3,238 m), and Forli (3,169 m). The Sciora mountains glowing in the evening are thrillingly beautiful.

82. Piz Badile, *3,308 m,* Piz Cengalo, *3,310 m*

This is the fifth day since I arrived in Vicosoprano along the Mera river. Remarkably, it has continued to snow in the middle of April. Whenever the snow began to abate I would go out to try and see the mountains, but it was impossible. After I had tried several times, it finally ceased to snow. Going down the Mera river I again came to the village of Soglio to photograph Piz Badile towering in the deep Val Bondasca. At six forty-five in the afternoon, just when I began to give up for the day I noticed a small ray of sun coming down. The sunlight increased and moved to Piz Badile and Piz Cengalo, until the two mountains were bathed in sunshine.

83. Engadin

I entered Engadin through Passo del Maloja after I had spent a night near Lago di Como in Italy. There were no people around in Maloja except a little girl and her brother who gazed at us while I photographed the mountains. Walking along the left bank of Lej da Sils, I found the village of Sils Maria on the right hand side a little way from the lake. Then there was Lej da Silvaplauna, divided into two with one section twice the size of the smaller one, called Lej da Champfer. I also noticed villages on the left named after each lake. I recommend going up the winding path through the middle of Piz Surlej to have the best view of local scenes with forests and lakes. It is even better in the morning when sunlight runs parallel to the slant of the mountainside and the crimson larches shine brightly.

84. Lej da Sils, Piz Sirlej, *3,188 m*

Our microbus drove slowly up the winding path to Val Bregaglia and ran smoothly after we had passed it. The road was level, the sky was deep blue, and the water of the lakes was transparently clear. There were no people to be seen in the town of St. Moritz and it was very calm and quiet. With our limited budget we had to stay in a camping ground outside the town of St. Moritz, which draws many elegant people in season. We were scolded by a watchman when we fished for trout in the lake for our dinner.

Dolomiti

This range is named after the rock "dolomite" from which it is formed, and it is part of the eastern Alps. It was once Austrian territory, and even now people use German and Italian together to name places and mountains making it confusing and very difficult to understand. Marmolada (3,344 m) is the highest peak in the Dolomiti range; and a sole glacier runs from its summit to the north. The principal mountains are Catinaccio, Latemar, Sasso Lungo, Gruppo di Sella, Le Tofane, Gruppo dei Cadini, Tre Cime di Lavaredo, Monte Pelmo, Civetta and San Martino. Every mountain has mysterious shapes peculiar to the Dolomites and each has grand rock walls startling in color.

85. Sasso Lungo, *3,181 m*

Passing by the feet of Bolozaqo and Catinaccio, we stayed overnight in a camp at Campitello, a town ahead of Canzei. Though it had been closed for the day, we begged to stay the night. We were all surprised the next morning to find that Sasso Lungo was right under our noses. We promptly began taking photos. The morning glow gradually faded away and its beams moved down. The crimson larches were at their peak and the sunlight brought the larch woods into relief. The effect was just perfect. After taking pictures I headed for Passo del Maloja, but I was not as impressed as I had been in the morning because man-made artifacts such as the lift and the mountain hut intruded into the scene.

86. Torri Vajolet, *2,813 m*

Torri Vajolet is situated in the Catinaccio mountain range (called Rosengarten in German) and stands next to Catinaccio. Why has it become so famous despite its low altitude? It is because three rock towers with unique shapes stand out in parallel and they are called the three sister peaks of Vajolet. Looking up at Torri Vajolet near the Vajolet hut, we can see many beautiful peaks that stretch out into the sky. The snow in the valley of Vajolet was unexpectedly deep and we fell into it. We heard sounds of a snowslide around the valleys, but we didn't let it bother us. When we were setting up the equipment under the Vajolet hut a changeable spring sky began its activity again, indicating doubtful weather to come.

87. Torri Vajolet, *2.813 m*

I walked around looking for new camera angles of Torri Vajolet, but the weather hadn't improved yet and the clouds over Torri Vajolet moved fast. I could faintly see the blue sky through the violently changing clouds, but it diminished. At last, I found a place amidst the dense woods where a clump of trees stood alone. I climbed up the steep slope of snow and set up a tripod. It took me a long time to press the shutter as the clouds had begun to move rapidly. But the rock walls of Catinaccio, Vajolet, and the morning clouds made a perfect view when caught by my camera.

88. Piz Ciovazzes (Gruppo di Sella), *2,828 m*

''Sella Gruppe'' in German and ''Gruppo di Sella'' in Italian are the names given to this group of mountains. These are a number of mountains with almost equal altitudes, clustered together. There is a mountain called ''Sella,'' which is the chief name for the entire range, and Piz Boe (3,141 m) is the highest of them all. But as Piz Boe looks out over the tableland, it is hard to take a good picture of it. We should set an angle somewhere where we can view its towering rock wall in order to catch its altitude. The rock-cliff of Ciavazzes, right under the Sellapass, loomed with overwhelming bulk, which rather weakened the effect of the mountain.

89. Marmolada, *3,342 m*

This is the highest of the Dolomiti Alps and has a single glacier. The north wall of the mountain, where the glacier flows, has a rather low slant; a ski lift operates close to its summit. In contrast, a grand view of that rock-cliff, which is as sheer as if chopped by an axe, ranges nearly four kilometers. No one was around Valle d'Ombretta and it was silent there near the end of autumn. We went further up to the alp of Marmolada and found it was surrounded by painfully dry air. When the morning sunlight beamed down on the rock-cliff the next day, it seemed that nature held us with gentleness.

90. Civetta, *3,218 m*

To the south-southwest of Cortina d'Ampezzo and about twenty kilometers away in a straight line, there is a group of mountains called Civetta. Uncommonly, in the Dolomites, the peaks of Civetta run along the south-southwest and can be sighted from far away. The range includes a number of walls famous for mountaineering and rock climbing.

To the west facing Alleghe, Le Grazie is a most advantageous lookout from which to view the forceful mountain of Civetta and it is better than the observatory made especially for Civetta on the way to Monte Pelmo. Both views are better in the afternoon sunlight.

91. Civetta, *3,218 m*

We left the camp ground early in the morning to photograph Sasso Lungo. The weather was utterly fickle and impossible to forecast. In addition the air grew hazy, making it impossible to photograph from the lookout on Civetta we had put so much time into finding. I was unconsciously comparing the weather to the last time I had come here. That day Civetta had been bathed in evening sunlight with the moon on the left and it was as beautiful as if the night was swallowed into the clear sky.

92. Monte Pelmo, *3,168 m*

Pelmo has a unique character among the Dolomiti mountains, which all have their own peculiar moods. In the Dolomiti mountain range several mountains gather and form a united structure, including many high peaks, but Pelmo is alone and has enough good qualities to be praised on its own merits. We have all the more difficulty in taking pictures of it; therefore, we tried various angles and changes in distance, but I have not produced a favorite one yet. I began to think that harmony with its surroundings would make the most of Pelmo just like this picture of a distant view taken at Sass Pordoi. I would like to think this strangely deserted mood reflects Pelmo's nature.

93. Tofana di Rozes, *3,224 m*

The Tofana mountain range, west-northwest of Cortina d'Ampezzo, includes Tofana di Mezzo, highest of all at 3,224 meters, Tofana di Dentro (3,238 m), and Tofana di Rozes. Since the cable car has been extended to the top of Mezzo, the interest of climbers is in going to Tofana di Rozes' south wall. Starting from Cortina d'Ampezzo for Passo di Falzorego, we can begin to see the magnificent rock formation on our right that is the Tofana di Rozes' south wall. To be worthy of the name, the rock wall is made of limestone with a reddish color. It takes five to six hours to climb to the summit of the south wall, which is classified as the fourth grade. In the case of the southeast wall, graded sixth, fifteen to sixteen hours are required for the climb.

94. Croda da Lago, *2,709 m*

Contrasting with the grand rock wall of the Tofana mountains, Croda da Lago, south-southeast of Cortina d'Ampezzo, consists of several unique rock towers. There is a small rock tower, called Cinque Torri, on a plateau across Rozes' south wall which has become famous among tourists. However, Croda da Lago is not so well known, though it is full of charm. Some might call Croda da Lago the unfortunate one, but I prefer this obscure mountain to the other. I feel as if I have the secret of it and nobody else knows about it. On my way back from Passo di Falzorego, I saw Lago, half of it bathed in evening sunlight and the other half veiled in shadow and it reminded me of the glamour of an old medieval castle.

95. Punta Nera, *2,846 m, Sorapiss, 3,205 m*

In a great mountain range west-southwest of Cortina d'Ampezzo, there are Punta Nera and Punta Sorapiss. Neighboring these two mountains, there is a mass of mountains which are heart-shaped. Their names are Gruppo delle Marmarole and Nateloo. Since it was off-season for traffic, we had to park our microbus at Lago di Misurina. In summer we could have gone as far as Rifugio Lavoredo. It took us five hours to reach Rifugio Auronzo by sled and skis, because I had borrowed shoes and the blisters which I had developed on my toes had broken open. Sorapiss viewed here at a distance has a very sharp look; its left peak is covered by a mountain in front of it. It gave us quite a different impression from the one we received at Lago di Misurina or at Cortina.

96. Gruppo dei Cadina (Cima Cadini), *2,839 m*

With Lago di Misurina in the center, Gruppo dei Cadini is confronted by Monte Cristallo and faces Tre Cime di Lavaredo on the north. It does not look very interesting from around Lago di Misurina, but as we go further toward the interior of Lavaredo country it begins to improve. In Rifugio Auronzo and Rifugio Lavaredo it comes into its own. The Cadini mountains range in height between 2,500 and 2,800 meters, They look attractive when snow is on the surface of the mountain rocks, which means that the view is best between fall and spring, rather than in the summer when it does not snow. But it is also true that Cadini in summer has its own charms which we cannot find any place else. In the foreground of Cadini flowers bloom all around Rifugio Lavaredo.

97. Monte Cristallo (Cima di Mezzo), *3,221 m*

The people of Cortina are very proud of Monte Cristallo, situated to the northeast of Cortina d'Ampezzo. The highest peak of this range is Cima di Mezza and there are two other mountains over 3,000 meters in elevation. One mountain, which has a lift right under the summit, is 3,036 meters and has been named Cristallino d'Ampezzo. We have promptly started photographing the surrounding mountain ranges, using the Olimpia camping ground as our base. On this day, we visited Valle di Landro near Dobbiaco, crossing over Lago di Misurina. On the way back from there by the same route, and soon after passing Passo di Tre Croci, an evening glow began over Monte Cristallo. Brightening to delicate red and yellow, the rock wall of Cristallo changed color moment by moment and grew dark quietly.

98. Monte Cristallo (Piz Popena), *3,152 m*

After passing Passo di Tre Croci, Monte Cristallo began to show us its full figure. This mountain is not as tall as that of Cima di Mezzo, and stands near Monte Mezzo though they are separated by the source of the Valfonda. I have taken many pictures of them, both individually and together, and they are a really good motif for me. The features of Popena change; closer to Lago di Misurina it begins to assert itself. Passing Valfonda, we can view the sharpened peak of Popena, which looks like the blade of a razor. If a cloud were added to it, it would be ideal. Anyhow, Popena always pleases me.